LAUGH, LOVE, AND LIVE WITH HAPPINESS

HOW TO LIVE A STRESS, ANXIETY, AND DEPRESSION-FREE LIFE?

DR. AMIT DAS

To

*All my bosses and students who made a difference in my professional
career.*

*"The health and happiness of an individual can be severely harmed by
stress. So, the people in your life should be a source of reducing
stress not causing more of it."*

- Dr. Amit Das, Motivational Speaker, Leadership Coach and Mentor.

Contents

Foreword

Dear Reader,

Our culture is plagued by stress, which leads to problems with relationships, physical disease, addictions, errors, inefficiency, lack of satisfaction, and unhappiness. This book examines the profound insight and inspiration we can derive from a stressful life, as well as how we can overcome all odds and rise like phoenixes. This book explains how to avoid tiredness and concern and nurture a mental attitude that will provide serenity and pleasure, starting with the fundamental information about stress, anxiety, and depression that one must understand and ending with tactics for evaluating it. This mini series edition book provides a thorough overview of the best coping mechanisms for mild to strong emotions. Anxiety-relieving techniques improve your awareness to prevent depression.

This book will also assist you in comprehending what stress is, its causes and consequences, the connections between stress and the body and mind, and the techniques for long-term alleviation. This book will assist you in lowering the stress in your life, regardless of how much you are currently under pressure. You can do this if you take the time to put what you learn into practise.

Get your copy today to get started on your stress, anxiety, and depression-reduction journey!

So, happy reading and learning to all my readers.

Carpe diem.

Dr. Amit Das

Motivational Speaker, Leadership Coach, and Mentor.

Preface

Modern life is filled with a variety of pressures and difficulties, including congested, noisy streets; pollution; job loss; a controlling partner; a demanding workplace; financial difficulties; and global pandemics. This book will show you how to quickly change your attitude from one of negativity to positivity, pinpoint the source of your stress, and then let it go so you may create your own happiness.

- *Are you someone who suffers from stress?*
- *Have you tried different things to resolve the problem, but nothing works?*
- *Are you ready to try a natural and simple solution that works?*

No matter how stressed you are right now, this book will help you reduce the tension in your life. If you take the time to put what you learn into practise, you can achieve this. You will enhance the lives of others around you as you make improvements in your own life. It's common for people to put off dealing with stress until it gets overwhelming; this is the wrong strategy. The book offers a thorough method for dealing with stress that respects the harmony, balance, and integration of the mind, body, spirit, and emotions.

Learn practical, science-based techniques for overcoming stress, and you should take immediate action to stop and reduce stress as soon as it manifests itself. Get this book right away to discover these strategies and how to use them!

PREFACE

Acknowledgements

At the outset, I will thank my family for supporting me throughout the journey of writing my book and encouraging me to live my dreams; my son has always been instrumental in giving his inspiration to complete the writing of this book. Despite the fact that I am listed as the author of this book, "LAUGH, LOVE, AND LIVE WITH HAPPINESS" would not have been published if I had depended entirely on my own talents. Creating this book required more than anything—it took a family of dedicated and caring people who were always prepared to lend a hand.

Writing a book while working full-time is no simple task, so I'd want to express my gratitude to my amazing coworkers who act as cheerleaders in equal measure. Thank you, too, to my students and clients for your patience and unflinching support while I worked on this book!

Thank you to everyone who has listened to me argue for doing everything you can to make your life, including your work life, more progressive. I appreciate everyone's assistance throughout the process. This book would not have been possible without each of you having had an impact on my life in some manner.

Lastly, I would like to thank all the people with whom I have been associated. You gave me power. I would like to thank Notion Press for publishing my book. Finally, thank you all for gifting your time to read this book.

I'd want to convey my heartfelt appreciation to the almighty God for bestowing his blessings and being so gracious.

CHAPTER ONE

Understanding Stress, Anxiety, And Depression

"We have to put our stress in perspective, replace negative thoughts with positive ones and be proud of our achievements, no matter how small."
-Anonymous

Stress will always find us, no matter who we are or what we accomplish in life.

It's normal to experience stress, anxiety or tension, and depression; it's just a characteristic of being human. Whether a situation is important or not, stressing about it is an indication that you are feeling and that your heart is beating.

How will you define your stress, anxiety, and depression?

Nobody in history can claim to have never experienced stress, anxiety, and depression. More often than you would imagine, stress and anxiety can be good for you. It can be a chance for you to increase your tolerance and endurance. Being able to rise again after a trying circumstance may make you more powerful, brave, and tough.

Stress is a typical bodily response to change that causes physical, emotional, and cognitive reactions. Stress is a typical human reaction that happens to everyone. The human body is really built such that it may feel stress and respond to it.

For instance, if you have a big test coming up, your body may work harder and remain awake longer as a result of a stress and anxiety reaction. But when stress and anxiety persist without respite or rest time, that become an issue.

> "Life will always include some level of stress and anxiety. Stressful events can help us learn and grow in ways that we otherwise wouldn't be able to if we respond to them constructively."

The most prevalent type of emotional problem is anxiety disorders, which may affect everyone. Moving to a new location, beginning a new career, or taking an exam can all cause anxiety. Although this kind of anxiety is unpleasant, it might spur you on to work harder and do better. Ordinary anxiety is a passing emotion that has little impact on day-to-day activities.

Your body reacts to changes or challenges both physically and psychologically (stressors). That is fear. Stress responses help your body acclimate to unfamiliar situations. Stress can keep us alert, inspired, and ready to avoid danger.

Anxiety is your body's normal response to stress. It is a feeling of fear or apprehension about what lies ahead. For instance, before a speech on the first day of class or a job interview, some people may feel anxious and concerned.

You could quit doing the activities you like to do because of this form of anxiety. You could be prevented from using an elevator, crossing the street, or, in severe circumstances, even leaving your house. The anxiousness will only become worse if not handled.

"Anxiety has varied effects on different people. Sometimes the feelings of dread and terror remain or get stronger over time."

If you suffer from an anxiety disorder, the dread could be there constantly. It may be quite painful and debilitating. However, excessive stress has a number of negative effects on our health, ranging from physical sickness to mental exhaustion. Stress is a normal and natural aspect of life. Promises of stress relief put individuals at risk of failure. The use of the term "stress-free" is still not recommended since the approach is permeated with an incorrect notion that will never materialise, even when utilised with the best of intentions and in conjunction with pertinent and advantageous thoughts and practises.

"Depression is a mental disorder characterised by a persistent feeling of melancholy and a loss of interest. Clinical depression, often referred to as major depressive disorder, has an impact on your emotions, thoughts, and behaviour and can result in a variety of mental and physical problems."

Depression is characterised by sadness and/or a loss of interest in former pastimes. The serious medical disease known as major depressive disorder, sometimes referred to as depression, commonly has an impact on a person's feelings, thoughts, and actions. Fortunately, it can also be treated.

Your life may be impacted by both people and situations that might create mental stress. Maybe these sayings serve as motivation for you to live the life of your dreams by removing tension from your life and thoughts.

Your body responds to demands and challenges by producing stress, which can be rather uncomfortable and debilitating. Stress may impair your performance at work and at home and cause a series of mental and physical issues.

Stress affects many of us, both at work and in our personal lives. Stress, like any other issue, necessitates a systematic strategy to overcome it, or at the very least manage it. There will be days when you'll feel completely stressed out, regardless of who you are, what you do, or how happy you believe you are. That said, it still isn't any simpler! When you're under a lot of stress, it might be difficult to envision a way out. Stress can feel overwhelming. Sometimes, all you truly need to get through a stressful situation is a gentle reminder that the end of the tunnel is in sight and that light is just around the corner.

> "*According to data on workplace stress, stress can result in decreased productivity, burnout, and conflicts at work. It can result in sadness, anxiety, and other severe mental health problems if left untreated.*"

Stress management training may help you deal with changes in a better way. You can struggle to do your routine daily duties, and you might periodically think life isn't worth living. However, you could have an anxiety disorder if your symptoms are severe, persistent for at least six months, and interfere with your life. Similarly, depression is more complicated than a simple case of the blues, and it doesn't suddenly "snap out" of you. For depression, long-term therapy may be required. But don't give up. Most depressed people experience better symptoms with medication, counselling, or both.

The stress, anxiety, and depression levels of Americans are among the highest in the world. According to data on workplace stress, stress can result in decreased productivity, burnout, and conflicts at work. It can result in sadness, anxiety, depression and other severe mental health problems if left untreated. The present human condition sadly includes stress, sadness, and worry. According to statistics, more and more people worldwide are battling mental health problems.

> *"Stress may cause significant declines in production, which end up costing both private businesses and governments a lot of money. These numbers on job stress have been gathered to demonstrate exactly how serious an issue it is."*

Whatever the level of stress, anxiety, and depression whether it be acute or chronic, it can affect your relationships and quality of life. Mental health illnesses, including anxiety, sadness, depression and rage difficulties, are the more complicated effects of high stress. Along with breathing exercises, the significance of self-care, mindfulness, and meditation, these will be covered in detail through practical activities.

At work, we're feeling more and more pressure. There isn't enough time, our supervisors bother us, and there is too much work. The psychological and financial implications of work-related stress are horrifying when things spiral out of control. The upheavals in the global economy that have reduced financial and job security are intimately related to these growing levels of workplace stress. This explains why a large number of people are converting to the gig economy.

Our world is being destroyed by the ego-driven lifestyle that the majority of people lead. Fortunately, altering our minds—or, more specifically, our connection with our minds—is the major factor in changing both ourselves and our surroundings in this way.

"Many people struggle with chronic stress, which can cause a variety of physical and mental health issues, including heart disease, anxiety, and depression. If you're one of the many people who feel overworked, stressed out, and overwhelmed , you're not alone."- Dr. Amit Das

CHAPTER TWO

Finding Root Causes, Signs, And Symptoms

"Stress, anxiety, and depression are caused when we are living to please others."
– Paulo Coelho

It can be quite tough to get back to your joyful mood once stress takes control.

Many of us have truly struggled to get to sleep at night because of unresolved issues that torment our brains. Most people make decisions and say things they later regret while acting impulsively. We frequently find ourselves in uncontrollable situations, which makes us vulnerable and upset.

According to the majority of experts, stress is the single biggest cause of all illnesses. We are continuously at war with this enemy in today's fast-paced society as a result of our anxiety to achieve more and more. Even though not all stress is negative and being worried or tense may sometimes be helpful, when it overwhelms only your stomach's butterflies or your brain's processing speed, it causes more strain than your heart can tolerate.

"You can either learn to deal with it and put it on your own in a happier and healthier area, or you can ignore it at your own risk. You can either deal with it and relocate it to a happier and healthier location, or you can ignore it at your peril."

Are you aware of the root causes, symptoms, and signs of your stress, anxiety, and depression?

Stress cannot be measured objectively using testing. A healthcare professional may use questionnaires to learn more about your stress and how it impacts your life. Emotional and mental symptoms brought on by stress include: Irritation or anxiety, depression, panic strikes, people who experience chronic stress frequently engage in harmful habits to cope with it, such as: Gambling, eating too much or getting an eating disorder, engaging in sexual activity, shopping, or internet browsing obsessively, smoking, drug abuse. Among the physical signs of stress are: Pains and aches, chest discomfort or a rushing heart sensation, fatigue or difficulty sleeping, difficulty having sex, and inadequate immune system etc.

Anxiety symptoms that have a reliable source include: It is difficult to manage worried thoughts or ideas restlessness, having trouble getting to sleep, fatigue, irritability, unaccounted-for aches and discomfort. Someone else's anxiety symptoms could not be the same as yours. It's crucial to understand the symptoms of anxiety because of this. Read about the many symptoms of anxiety that you could encounter. If you think you could be suffering from a heart attack or a mental health emergency while having a panic attack, the symptoms might worsen. The concern that you could receive unfavourable judgement if you experience a panic attack in front of others is another prevalent phobia that can make the condition worse. The symptoms of panic attacks might vary widely from person to person.

You could have panic disorder if you frequently have panic or anxiety episodes. The precise source of anxiety is unclear to experts. However, it's possible that a number of elements interact. Anxiety may be brought on by: Additional medical conditions, including diabetes or depression, first-degree relatives suffering from a phobia, environmental issues, including child maltreatment, usage of drugs, and scenarios like surgery or workplace danger. Additionally, scientists think it originates from the parts of the brain in charge of managing fear as well as memory storage and retrieval for emotional and fear-related experiences.

Numerous factors can lead to stress. One significant circumstance or incident in your life may be the cause of your stress. Or it may be the accumulation of several little things. Because of this, it could be more difficult for you to pinpoint the source of your stress or to explain it to others.

Depression may run in families due to genetics. For instance, if one identical twin develops depression, there is a 70% probability that the other will also get the condition at some point in life. It seems that those who have low self-esteem, are easily stressed out, or are usually gloomy are more prone to suffering from depression. Although you might only experience depression once in your lifetime, most people experience many bouts. Many depressed individuals often have symptoms that are severe enough to interfere with daily activities, including jobs, school, social interactions, or interpersonal relationships.

Abuse on the physical, sexual, or emotional levels can increase your risk of depression in later life. Other elements, like living alone and lacking social support, might exacerbate certain medicines. Conflict. Some medications, including the acne medication isotretinoin, the antiviral medication interferon-alpha, and corticosteroids, can raise your chance of developing depression.

Since depression is considered to be a complicated characteristic, it is more likely that there are several small-effect genes at play than a single gene that increases the chance of developing the condition. Like in other mental disorders, the genetics of depression is not as clear-cut or easy as it is in diseases that are solely hereditary, like Huntington's chorea or cystic fibrosis.

Depression can result from happy life events like beginning a new job, graduating, or getting married. Moving, losing a job or source of money, divorcing, or retirement can also do this. However, a "natural" reaction to stressful life situations is never the clinical depressive syndrome. More personal issues clinical depression can be brought on by issues like social isolation brought on by other mental conditions or being rejected by a family or social group.

Sometimes a serious disease co-occurs with depression, and other illnesses can sometimes cause depression. Nearly 30% of individuals who struggle with drug abuse also have significant or clinical depression. Even though alcohol or narcotics momentarily improve your mood, they ultimately worsen depression. Intense anxiety or panic sensations that are directly attributed to a physical health issue are included in anxiety disorders that are caused by medical conditions.

You could feel stressed if you feel a lot of pressure. You face significant life changes, concern yourself with anything, don't have much or any influence over how a scenario will turn out, have obligations that feel daunting, you lack sufficient jobs, activities, or life change, you encounter hatred, bigotry, or abuse, and are undergoing a time of uncertainty.

Anxiety and worry about things that are commonplace or usual, as well as persistent and excessive anxiety, are symptoms of generalised anxiety disorder. The worry is excessive compared to the situation, hard to regulate, and has an impact on how you physically feel. It frequently co-occurs with depression or other anxiety disorders.

High degrees of anxiety, dread, and avoidance of social settings are symptoms of social anxiety disorder (social phobia), which are brought on by emotions of humiliation, self-consciousness, and worry about being evaluated or perceived adversely by others. Major anxiety when exposed to a particular object or scenario and a desire to avoid it are characteristics of certain phobias. Some people experience panic episodes due to phobias. Intense anxiety or panic symptoms that are a direct result of drug abuse, prescription use, toxic chemical exposure, or drug withdrawal are the hallmarks of substance-induced anxiety disorder.

Stress burnout has a variety of reasons. Ironically, even though so many of us aim for professional success, it can occasionally cause serious issues. For instance, our work schedules may be the most important component in this situation. The Organization for Economic Cooperation and Development reports that Mexico, South Korea, and Greece are the top three countries in the world for the number of hours worked annually per person, all of which exceed 2,000. Among the main industrialised nations, US workers put in the most hours—more than 1,700 hours a year. Of course, a sizable fraction of them work several jobs and put in an average of over 40 hours every week. Thus, burnout is probably not all that surprising.

The fit between jobs, or how well your interests and talents correspond with what you really do, is the last work-related aspect to think about. You guessed right. High stress is caused by low fitness. In order to find positions that truly reflect who you are, you must take action over the long term. Continuing with the non-work portion of the equation I want you to start by considering the calibre of your most important connections. That mostly consists of family and close friends. The tough sensation it produces when those relationships are strained will accompany you to work and weigh on how you feel. The robustness of your identity outside of work is another consideration.

Excessive anxiety may be brought on by a major incident or a pile of less stressful life circumstances, such as a loss in the family, work stress, or persistent financial worries. personality. Anxiety disorders are more likely to affect some personality types than others. Each person has unique stressors.

It becomes a different issue if the unemployed individual finds work but is nevertheless plagued by the fear of being fired once more. Their fear has taken over their life and has become chronic. Perhaps they are afraid of losing their jobs and feel the need to preserve money, which makes them no longer want to go out with friends. Perhaps they insist on leading such a simple life that it borders on the absurd and damages their relationships with others around them.

While it may be nearly impossible to avoid stress, this does not mean that you must accept the fact that you will always be under stress. Stress not only makes life difficult, but it also raises your risk of developing a number of illnesses, including heart disease, high blood pressure, and even stroke. This means that being able to manage stress well is crucial. Every single one of us has experienced stress at some point or another. Stress actually comes and goes in our lives frequently, maybe even without our notice. When stress is at its worst, it may completely upend our lives and cause significant problems like mental breakdowns and even deadly heart attacks.

Finally, I have to emphasise your physical health. I won't go into great detail on this topic beyond stating that food, exercise, and sleep all have a significant impact on possible burnout. This entails consuming more fresh meals and fewer unhealthy fats; engaging in regular exercise to keep one's energy levels up; and getting at least seven to eight hours of sleep each night.

"You will face numerous obstacles, and there is no quick fix, but you have the power to overcome any challenge, so stop leading an unpleasant and miserable existence. You may better handle stress , anxiety, and depression in your life with the aid of the useful knowledge in this book. The information era has made life more challenging than we could have ever anticipated."-Dr. Amit Das

Measuring Your Stress, Anxiety, And Depression

"You don't have to see the whole staircase, just take the first step."
— Martin Luther King

Evaluate your current levels of stress, anxiety, and depression so that you can do to create an effective coping mechanism.

Our lives may include stress, which may have both positive and harmful impacts. Our perception of an event, a change, or an issue is what essentially controls the stress reaction. It might be difficult to find balance in our lives and control our stress. Recognising the extent to which our lives are impacted by stress is a crucial first step before pursuing measures to reduce it. The following self-assessment measures may be used to gauge our level of stress, the sort of stress we are feeling, and how effectively our stress management techniques are functioning.

Self Evaluation:1

Depending on how closely each statement describes your present way of life, rank each statement from 1 (always applies to you) to 5 (never applies to you).

- I never whine about time squandered or the past.
- I am the right weight for my height.
- I have a support system of friends, family, and acquaintances.
- I am generally in good health.
- I am able to speak openly about my feelings when I am under pressure.
- I can recognise when I am not coping well under pressure.
- I can express my emotions honestly when I'm furious, stressed out, or scared.
- I engage in enjoyable activities at least once every week.
- I spend time by myself during the day.
- I often have cordial discussions with my roommates regarding domestic topics like housework, money, and day-to-day concerns.
- Never do I try to do everything on my own.
- I have good time management skills, which means I can organise things properly.
- I have at least one neighbour I can ask a favour of.
- I get 7 to 8 hours of sleep at least 5 nights a week.
- I work out till I start sweating at least three times a week.
- My salary or income is sufficient to cover my essential needs.
- I get to and from work in less than an hour each day.
- I don't get upset when I have to wait, get stopped in traffic, or be late for an appointment.

Interpretaion of Test Scores: <30=Red Zone; 31-50=Orange Zone; 51-70=Yellow Zone; >70-90= Green Zone

Self Evaluation: 2

On a scale of 0 to 10, where 0 represents being completely depleted and 10 represents being totally charged up, note how charged or enthusiastic you feel in each area. There are variances between the questions despite the fact that some of them are identical, so you should approach each one individually. It is best to respond quite promptly. Instead of attempting to quantify how many times you felt a certain emotion, suggest the option that sounds like a reasonable approximation.

- How likely are you to actively look for knowledge about an unexpected, unfavourable occurrence and how to deal with it?
- How much influence do you have over family decisions?
- How much influence over decisions do you actually have at work? (If you aren't now employed outside the house, base your response on your most recent position.)
- How much do you think that things that happen in your life are really luck, fate, or chance?
- What is your best estimate of the quantity and calibre of communication you experienced with your parents just after birth?
- How closely do you feel a part of your idea of a higher power or of a noble cause?
- How much do you think your life has meaning?
- How much interaction do you have with groups that you would classify as spiritual?
- How often do you engage in a really calming activity?

- How frequently do you practise a spiritual discipline to enliven your inner life, such as prayer, meditation, or inspiring reading?
- Which of the following best sums up how you drink?
- How much do you think you've previously managed to deal effectively with?
- How certain are you that you can restrain your emotions under pressure?
- How often do you think of a bad situation as transient rather than permanent when things aren't going well?
- To what extent was your mother's calm and usually accommodating during your early years?
- How quickly can you make friends in an unfamiliar setting?
- How likely are you to ask friends or family for assistance while under a lot of stress?
- How frequently do you perceive individuals as hostile, uncooperative, or exploitative compared to other people?
- How frequently do you question what people's motives are for you?
- How much do you know about practical, healthy methods to unwind?
- What percentage of the time do you overstate the significance of terrible things that happen to you?
- How likely are you to concentrate on the parts of a complicated situation that you can control while you're under stress?
- How well are you able to alter your thoughts when under a lot of stress?
- How likely are you to stand back and let things happen in a tense scenario as opposed to taking control?

- Which of the following actions are you most likely to take after you've reached the point of complete frustration?
- How likely would you be to send back a piece of clothing if you wore it for one day only to discover it was defective?
- How often do you engage in moderate exercise?
- How frequently do you have a sound night's sleep?
- How much energy do you have left for your work and daily activities?
- How close to the optimal weight range is your current weight?
- What percentage of your diet is wholesome?
- Which of the following statements best sums up your cigarette use?

Self Evaluation:3
Stress, Anxiety, and Depression - (SAD)Assesssment
Consider how you've been feeling over the past two weeks as you answer each question.

- How frequently has excessive stress about various things troubled you?
- How often has it concerned you that you can't unwind?
- How often has it affected you to be so antsy that it is difficult to sit still?
- How often has it worried you that you are irritated or quickly annoyed?
- How frequently has the fear that something bad could happen disturbed you?
- Have any of the following, such as being overweight, enjoying yourself sexually, making financial plans, etc., worried you?

- How frequently have you felt sad, depressed, or hopeless disturbed you?
- How frequently do you find yourself performing tasks with little interest or enjoyment?
- How frequently does it annoy you when you have problems falling or staying asleep or when you sleep too much?
- How frequently has being exhausted or lacking energy upset you?
- How frequently has an insufficient appetite or overeating disturbed you?
- How frequently have you felt inferior to yourself, like a failure, or like you have let your family or yourself down?
- How frequently has it disturbed you to have problems focusing on activities like reading the newspaper or watching television?
- How frequently has being fidgety or restless caused you to move about more than usual? Or how about speaking or moving so slowly that others may have noticed?
- Have you ever had a panic or fright attack due to anxiety?
- How frequently does it annoy you when you feel tense, frightened, or on edge?
- How frequently has worrying that you can't stop or control upset you?

Self Evaluation:4

Please read each statement and give it a score from 1 to 5, indicating how much it applied to you over the past several weeks. There are no correct or incorrect responses. Do not linger too long on any one sentence.

- It was difficult for me to unwind.
- I noticed that my mouth was dry and that I couldn't feel well at all.
- I also had trouble breathing (excessively quick breathing, dyspnea without physical activity, etc.).
- I had a hard time taking the initiative since I tended to overreact to things.
- I shook (especially in my hands), felt like I was expending a lot of anxious energy, and worried about scenarios when I would freak out and embarrass myself.
- I felt like I had nothing to look forward to, which made me agitated and made it difficult for me to unwind.
- I also felt depressed and blue.
- I was intolerant of anything that prevented me from moving on with what I was doing, felt on the verge of panic, was unable to feel excited about anything, thought little of myself personally, and thought I was pretty touchy.
- In the lack of physical effort, I was aware of my heart's activity (e.g. sense of heart rate increase, heart missing a beat).
- Without any justification, I felt afraid and life seemed pointless.

Interpretaion of Test Scores: <20=Red Zone; 21-30=Orange Zone; 31-40=Yellow Zone; >40-50= Green Zone

"It might be challenging to know what to do when you're stressed out and not quite yourself. To assist you in assessing your levels of stress, anxiety, or depression and determining whether learning any particular strategy may help you feel better."- Dr. Amit Das

CHAPTER FOUR

Learning To Relax And Live A Happy Life

"Everyone, whether they have an anxiety, stress, or depression illness, or are simply going through a stressful time, needs a little motivation from time to time in life."
-Dr. Amit Das

Nothing is permanent in this world, neither happiness nor trouble.

The ultimate objective is to live a balanced life that includes time for work, relationships, leisure, and fun as well as the fortitude to withstand stress and face obstacles head-on. I sincerely hope that this chapter will be a steadfast source of support for you, especially in difficult times.

"The most effective instrument in the world is the mind. Modify your thinking. And you'll alter your way of life."

This is a thorough guide that focuses on stress, anxiety, and depression reduction and relaxation. You might believe that only severe illnesses or severe bodily or mental injuries can lead to stress or depression. That is untrue. Even pure delight, being in a draught, or crossing a busy junction might partially activate the body's stress response systems. Since stress or anxiety may be caused by any emotion or action, it's not even necessary that tension is unhealthy for you; in fact, it's the spice of life.

> "*In order to handle stress effectively, we have to accept that stress is part of life, accept that we cannot control everything and maintain a positive attitude.*"

Regardless of your age, you may adopt and use the SAD (Stress, Anxiety, and Depression) management techniques in this chapter. With these easy techniques, dealing with SAD is no longer a problem but rather a given. Here are mentioned different activities you can do to unwind and lower your "SAD" level.

- Being mindful might increase your productivity in today's hectic society. It eases tension, sharpens attention, and enhances your capacity to overcome obstacles at home and at work. With consistent practice, mindfulness may alter the path of your life. When we are in a state of mindfulness, we are able to observe what is happening in the here and now without passing judgement.
- One of the most important abilities is time management, whether we're talking about business or life in general. Stress levels will increase if you let your day run haphazardly rather than consciously planning it. It also makes it too easy for other people to interrupt you. You'll increase productivity and reduce stress if you

work for around 90% of the time and take breaks for approximately 10% of the time. Most individuals believe that putting in long hours of work will result in greater productivity. Typically, that is not true.

"When everything seems to be going against you, remember that the airplane takes off against the wind, not with it."-Henry Ford

- We frequently believe that accomplishing an easy activity before beginning the difficult work would help us gain some momentum. Actually, no. Starting with a simple activity encourages you to do other simple activities, which ultimately serves as an escape from the work that you see as stressful.
- Don't keep your sentiments to yourself when life overwhelms you. Tell everything to a family member or someone you can trust. Consult a counsellor if required. Verbalizing your emotions is said to help over time lessen feelings of emotional overload when you come across upsetting circumstances.
- Knowing that you have little control over your circumstances frequently causes stress and worry. Accept that there are certain things you cannot control in order to lessen these emotions, and instead concentrate on finding effective solutions for the components that you can manage.

"Sometimes the bad things that happen in our lives put us directly on the path to the most wonderful things that will ever happen to us."-Nicole Reed

- Stress has an effect on the body as a whole in addition to the brain. Similar to this, a healthy body and mind go hand in hand. Five minutes of aerobic exercise, according to experts, may be all it takes to reduce anxiety.
- Comedy therapy laughter causes the body to physically shift, boosts endorphin levels, and stimulates the heart, lungs, and muscles. All of which aid in lowering the unpleasant bodily effects of stress. Watching a comedy show or your favourite comic can make you chuckle.
- The brain cells can obtain enough protein during sleep to support development and repair the harm done by stress and other conditions. A healthy emotional state cannot be sustained without adequate sleep. Get eight to nine hours of sleep every night, and you'll start to notice a change in how anxious you are.

"We all have anxiety about things. We all have little insecurities, but eventually you have to face your fears if you want to be successful, and everybody has some fear of failure."-Nick Saban

- Positive affirmations can assist relax the mind by shifting the emphasis away from the troubling scenario you are facing. Our ideas exacerbate tension and worry.
- Be gentle with yourself because perfection is a pipe dream. Concentrate on the things you can control. Recognize and appreciate your accomplishments, no matter how minor. Refrain from taking things personally.
- Make the switch to a standing desk and have meetings outside. While making or receiving calls, move about. Use your fitness band to log 10,000 steps.

"If we wanted to change the situation, we first had to change ourselves. And to change ourselves effectively, we first had to change our perceptions."-Stephen Covey

- Stop concentrating on what you lack rather than what you do have. Avoiding watching television advertising is the simplest method to cease dwelling on your needs.
- Use meditation to help you clear your mind. Cook, garden, experiment with origami, dance, or read. Just take deep breaths in and out while keeping an eye on the clock's needle. Stay present and clear your mind. My preferred stress-relieving workout is to lean against a wall.
- Quit whining about things that are beyond your control. Being human gives us the unique opportunity to experience all that life has to offer, good, terrible, and ugly. To live a stress-free life, one must develop coping mechanisms.

"People become attached to their burdens sometimes more than the burdens are attached to them."-George Bernard Shaw

- Keeping or altering your point of view It's normal to feel overwhelmed when you're going through a difficult moment. Even while it may seem that taking control of a challenging circumstance is the best course of action, there are occasions when letting go may help you maintain your mental health.
- Compose a card for someone you care about. Regardless of who it is, I can guarantee that they will value a card letting them know you are thinking of them. This type of impromptu generosity is good for both you and the

person who is the recipient. Making someone else feel happy may make you feel good, and doing these things has been shown to boost the mood of people with social anxiety.

- Observing the difference you make in that person's life can also make you feel better about yourself, which helps reduce stress. Visit a free gallery or museum. Cultural institutions provide a safe haven of constructive distraction, reducing stress and stimulating our creativity. Check out what's available in your neighbourhood to see if you may sometimes obtain free access or discounted fees.

"If you can't fly, run. If you can't run, walk. If you can't walk, crawl, but by all means, keep moving."- Martin Luther King.Jr.

- Stop dwelling on the past and future and start living in the present. Being in your body and experiencing your emotions are two aspects of being present in the moment that many people truly struggle with.
- Do not multitask. It makes sense why we're all so stressed out while we're concurrently responding to texts, watching TV, and talking on the phone. In addition to being completely ineffective, multitasking has been shown to boost the levels of the stress chemicals cortisol and adrenaline, which can cause your body to go into panic mode.
- Refrain from accepting tasks more than you can handle. Being overly busy is a problem. In fact, slowing down may be scary because it makes you aware of your emotions and makes you experience them.

"Anxiety was born in the very same moment as mankind. And since we will never be able to master it, we will have to learn to live with it— just as we have learned to live with storms."-Paulo Coelho

- Grab an embrace. Hugging produces oxytocin, which decreases stress chemicals like cortisol and raises serotonin levels, which are connected to happiness.
- You can create coping mechanisms and organise your feelings with the aid of a mental health expert. They might also develop into a place where you feel comfortable and supported while you work on a concrete strategy to get through challenging circumstances.
- Dwelling on your annoyance with a circumstance, person, place, or object that cannot be altered just serves to depress you. You alone are the only one who will eventually determine how to react to what is. Your life is not someone else's life. Life is what it is.

"There is only one way to happiness and that is to cease worrying about things which are beyond the power of our will."-Epictetus

- When you let go of tension, develop a relationship with your body, mind, and soul, and just be yourself without inhibition, amazing things happen. Life itself actually slows down. You give up making plans for the weekend. You cease anticipating wonderful occasions. You start to feel like a human being as you learn to live in the present. You just enjoy riding the wave of life while feeling happy and pleased. You move with ease, steadiness, composure, and gratitude. A new viewpoint emerges as a curtain is raised. And this is how you lead a life free of tension.

- When navigating these trying moments, reaching out to the community or close ones for support, incorporating healthy rituals into your routine, allowing yourself to experience all your emotions, and getting professional assistance may all be crucial measures.
- Treat people the way you want to be treated. Not everyone will treat you in the manner in which you would want to be treated. When you treat people with compassion, love, and respect, you will experience deep levels of inner serenity.

"We ourselves feel that what we are doing is just a drop in the ocean. But the ocean would be less because of that missing drop."- Mother Teresa

- You will face numerous obstacles, and there is no quick fix, but you have the power to overcome any challenge, so stop leading an unpleasant and miserable existence.
- Refrain from adopting other people's issues. The fact that they aren't your problems is the main benefit of other people's troubles. You develop the habit of enabling when you take on other people's issues on a regular basis.
- Quitting overanalyzing hypothetical situations is the first step to living a stress-free existence. It's easy to get caught up in the realm of worst-case scenarios.

"Happiness is not a brilliant climax to years of grim struggle and anxiety. It is a long succession of little decisions simply to be happy in the moment."-J. Donald Walters

- Assume a yoga position. Several yoga postures may be attempted at home to aid with anxiety reduction. Sit on your knees, lean forward until your face is resting on the floor, and keep your arms at your sides to attempt the child's position. This soothing position encourages us to spend some time alone and calms our busy brains.
- Listen to a book on audio. It is quite soothing and a cosy way to unwind before bed to be told a tale. There are a large variety of podcasts available online, and it takes considerably less effort than reading to listen to them. Make your home a refuge of safety. Make your bedroom a tranquil retreat by decorating it accordingly!
- Give social media a rest. Despite the potential that connectivity and social media provide us, utilising them excessively might have negative effects. It might make you feel less confident about yourself, distract you from the present, and add drama to your life. Take a break because all of these things contribute to stress.

"Life isn't perfect—on any front—and the most we should ask of ourselves or anybody else is to do what we can with what we have. On some days, doing the best we can may still fall short of what we would like to be able to do. When you feel overwhelmed, keep in mind that little by little is how things get accomplished. One item, one undertaking, and one instant at a time."- Dr. Amit Das

About The Author

Dr. Amit Das, is a renowned executive advisor, consultant, educationist, author, speaker, counsellor, and coach whose 25+ years of business experience provides high-impact, practical solutions that support his clients' leadership development and organisational transformations. He worked for three great fortune 500 MNCs and left rich leagacy of organising transformational learning workshops. He has transformed more than 3500+ working executives through his path breaking soft skills training workshops. Dr. Amit Das is recognised as an innovative, principled thought leader who combines intellectual rigor and discipline with an ability to translate theory into practice. His operational skills are coupled with a strategic ability to analyse, develop, and implement successful strategies for profitability, growth, and sustainability.

Dr. Amit Das has a successful track record in aligning learning and training solutions to key business strategy with a strong focus on flawless execution excellence to facilitate individual, business divisional, and organisational performance. He keeps relentless focus on measuring training impact and ROI, people capability building graphs, training process governance, performance coaching, and strategic thinking. These have been some of his key individual success traits. His core capabilities include performance coaching, designing training and development frameworks, psychometric assessment and analysis, competency framework development and assessments, content design and facilitation of soft skills and leadership programmes, Learning Management Systems, Learning Impact Measurement, Talent Analysis, and Performance Coaching and Counselling.

Dr. Amit Das has authored multiple management and self-development books, like Create Your Leadership Edge, Building Organisational Capability, Ethical Road Map, Attomic Attention, BYPB, Implementor, ALOUD, Redefining Talent Management, Defining Your Success Factors, Lead or Plead, Make The Most Of Your Life, Better Half or Bitter Half, Organisational Transformation Through Learning, The Transformative Mind & Soul are few of them.

He has a Ph.D. and a Fellowship in strategic learning, along with his first class degrees in Human Resource Management, Marketing Management, International Business, and Corporate Laws from the top business schools in India. He is a certified Psychometric analyst, HR Metrics, OD Interventionist, Human Psychologist, Lifecoach, Leadership Developer, Black Belt (LSS), Strategic Thinker, Talent Analyst, certified professional trainer from the U.K. and certified behavioral coach from the U.S.A.

Dr. Amit Das likes googling, reading books, writing articles & books, cooking, listening to old melodies, and counselling people to unleash their true potential to build a strong nation. He is married and blessed with a son. He would love to hear about your experience after reading his books. You can email him and share your thoughts, or you can use his services for life coaching, positive behavioural counseling, educational support, and mentoring for young, promising students pursuing their B.B.A. and M.B.A. degrees.

References

- *Stress Management: Simple Techniques to Kill Your Anxiety and Be Happy (Reduce Your Depression While Seeing Your Life in a New Light) Kindle Edition by James Crawford (Author).*
- *How to Stop Worrying and Start Living: Time-Tested Methods for Conquering Worry Paperback – 1 August 2016 by Dale Carnegie.*
- *Mind It... Realizations & Solutions Blanking The (Thinking) Worries: An Ideal book for Life, Mind & Stress Management in English Perfect Paperback – 31 December 2020 by A. T. Rajkumar (Author).*
- *Stress Cure Now: A Stress Management Book With A New, Logical And Effective Approach Kindle Edition by Sarfraz Zaidi MD.*
- *The Courage To Be Disliked: How to free yourself, change your life and achieve real happiness (Courage To series) Hardcover – 30 April 2018 by Ichiro Kishimi and Fumitake Koga (Author).*
- *The Everyday Hero Manifesto Paperback – 15 September 2021 by Robin Sharma.*
- *Stress Management: Simple Techniques to Kill Your Anxiety and Be Happy (Reduce Your Depression While Seeing Your Life in a New Light) by James Crawford | 9 May 2022.*
- *Stress Management: A Comprehensive Handbook of Techniques and Strategies Hardcover – Import, 13 August 2002 by Jonathan C. Smith.*
- *Time to Decompress: A Guide to Self-Healing with Stress (Stress Management books Book 1) Kindle Edition by*

David Benson.

- *The Stress Management Book: Expert Strategies for Dealing With Stress for Men, Women, Teens & Kids Kindle Edition by Brian Shawn.*
- *Art of Stress Management (Rupa Quick Reads) Kindle Edition by Sarvesh Gulati.*
- *Getting Things Done, Paperback – 22 April 2015 by David Allen.*
- *Ikigai: The Japanese secret to a long and happy life Hardcover – 27 September 2017 by Héctor García (Author), Francesc Miralles (Author).*
- *The Mayo Clinic Guide to Stress-Free Living Paperback – Illustrated, 24 December 2013 by Amit Sood (Author), Mayo Clinic (Author.*
- *Stop Overthinking: 23 Techniques to Relieve Stress, Stop Negative Spirals, Declutter Your Mind, and Focus on the Present (The Path to Calm Book 1) Kindle Edition by Nick Trenton (Author).*
- *Stress-Free Productivity: A Personalised Toolkit to Become Your Most Efficient, Creative Self Paperback – Import, 3 March 2022 by Dr Alice Boyes (Author).*
- *Delete Stress and Pain on the Spot! Paperback – Import, 18 July 2021 by Dr Kam Yuen (Author), Marnie Greenberg (Author).*
- *Guide to Stress Free Living: How to Live Stress-Free and Relax Paperback – Illustrated, 25 May 2014 by David Blaine (Author).*
- *365 Days With Self-Discipline: 365 Life-Altering Thoughts on Self-Control, Mental Resilience, and Success (Simple Self-Discipline Book 5) Kindle Edition by Martin Meadows (Author).*
- *What Happened to You?: Conversations on Trauma, Resilience, and Healing Paperback – 1 July 2021 by Oprah*

Winfrey (Author), Dr Bruce Perry.

- *Live the Let-Go Life Study Guide: Breaking Free from Stress, Worry, and Anxiety Paperback – 31 October 2017 by Joseph Prince (Author).*
- *Clear Your Mind: Proven Techniques to Relieve Stress, Stop Negative Spirals, Declutter Your Mind, and Focus on the Present Kindle Edition by Paul Carter (Author) Format: Kindle Edition.*
- *Anger Management: How to Control Anger, Master Your Emotions, and Eliminate Stress and Anxiety, including Tips on Self-Control, Self- Discipline, NLP, and Emotional Intelligence Hardcover – Import, 10 January 2020 by Steven Turner (Author).*
- *How To Avoid Burnout: a guide on how to fix an epidemic of stress Kindle Edition by Olivia Davies (Author), Olivia Davies (Author) Format: Kindle Edition.*
- *Stressilient : How to Beat Stress and Build Resilience Paperback – Import, 10 June 2022 by Dr Sam Akbar (Author).*
- *The End of Stress: Four Steps to Rewire Your Brain Paperback – 23 September 2014 by Don Joseph Goewey.*
- *Heal Yourself From That Depression: A Self-Guided Book On How To Heal Yourself From Depression When Nobody Else Can Kindle Edition by Wanda Samuels (Author).*
- *Stress Simplified: A Guide to Controlling and Reducing Stress Effectively Paperback – 16 July 2021 by Guru(Author).*
- *The Stress Management Handbook: A Practical Guide to Staying Calm, Keeping Cool, and Avoiding Blow-Ups Paperback – Import, 17 March 2020 by Eva Selhub M.D. (Author).*

www.ingramcontent.com/pod-product-compliance
Lightning Source LLC
Chambersburg PA
CBHW032023140726
47988CB00017BA/1488